————  ————

Dear Addiction

Cease and Desist

————  ————

Patra Ann Smith

ISBN 978-1-64471-318-1 (Paperback)
ISBN 978-1-64471-319-8 (Digital)

Copyright © 2019 Patra Ann Smith
All rights reserved
First Edition

All rights reserved. No part of this publication may be reproduced, distributed, or transmitted in any form or by any means, including photocopying, recording, or other electronic or mechanical methods without the prior written permission of the publisher. For permission requests, solicit the publisher via the address below.

Covenant Books, Inc.
11661 Hwy 707
Murrells Inlet, SC 29576
www.covenantbooks.com

Introduction

In this book, you'll journey with a friend through her addiction story. You'll see how her addiction started, what caused it, and understand what fears held her there. You'll see her struggle to break free, and you'll go with her to her ultimate rock bottom where she came face-to-face with the entity behind her addiction in a struggle for her life. Most importantly, you'll learn what saved her life and what day-to-day practices continue to keep her living a sober fulfilling lifestyle. Her story may relate to yours in some way. Through that relation, you'll be able to see that *all* relationships with drugs and alcohol are traps that disguise themselves as a friend, at times, a frenemy that came to rob you of your life's purpose. Your story may be different from hers; but addiction has the same motives with everyone it attaches itself to which is to strip us of the divine seed planted in each of us by God, a seed that was meant to flourish into our own unique life's calling. What would want to strip you of your life's purpose and why? Something that knows the talent and power that is within you and the life changing effect it will have on others in your life's path because your life purpose coincides with God's plan!

So journey with Patra through this short story, her trials and triumph over sobriety, in hopes of being inspired to break free from any strong holds or fears in your own life that may be holding you back from living in your life's purpose.

This booklet is also a great workshop for readers who are struggling with addictions of their own and who are ready to start taking the necessary steps to begin their own journey to a life of sustained sobriety. The workshop will lead the reader to write their very own personalized cease and desist letter to addiction.

Letter to Addiction

Dear addiction,

Where did you come from? Genetics, learned behavior, maybe even a curse? I don't quite know! But I'd always ask myself, *Why did you choose me? Why am I so unlucky compared to everyone else?* Seemed like everyone else has the luxury of balancing their everyday life while still maintaining their nightly ritual of winding down with cocktail or ending their stressful workweek with a boozed-up weekend to make it all worthwhile.

But not me though. I could never just casually have a drink then get back to my regularly scheduled program. The drinks would quickly become my regularly scheduled program. I'd sometimes think, *Maybe I'm doing it all wrong!* So I'd try different drinking formulas. I remember trying to set a cutoff number for myself one night before I went out. I'd plan to stop drinking at three drinks that night no matter what. I was sure I found the solution to avoid drinking out of control. I went out; and after those three drinks, all the logic I'd worked out so perfectly before dissolved. It was like something else had hijacked my brain. I was no longer in the driver's seat of my thoughts or actions. That hijacker had its own plans for me. My logic changed. I began to think, *Three drinks were nothing! I'm definitely going to need more than that to really let my hair down and have some fun.*

Every now and then, a logical thought would try to interject to remind me of the previous pact I set with myself to only have three drinks; but addiction would bring a new logic to the table saying, "You set that cutoff number all wrong. Don't you see? You're not even tipsy yet. You know that you have a higher tolerance for alcohol than the average person!" That lie somehow made sense to me; and it was all I needed to kick off a boozed-up evening, with no brakes to stop. In fact, my new limit was "drink until you felt you had to much." And by that time, it was too late all together. My original plan had failed that night. Something else surely took the driver's seat, and it's clear now that it was you, addiction. I was unknowingly doomed from the first drink.

I was beginning to discover there is no perfect formula for drinking for an addict—except not using at all. Addiction, your best asset was your ability to keep yourself hidden to remain undiscovered. You had a way of deflecting the spotlight away from you. I'd blame everyone and everything else for my drinking; but, addiction, you remained blameless. It took me a long painful road to arrive at the truth that it was an addiction that caused all of this destruction in my life. It wasn't past pains or present failures, and it wasn't because of what others had done to me. I have an addiction! Everyone has deep-rooted issues and past trauma. But I partnered my problems with drug abuse, and that's what made every issue so life-ruining and impossible to get past.

In fact, addiction, you would play those past pains on a broken record to give yourself relevance. I've gotten many hints that point out I had an addiction. It has even been spelled out to me, but you had a way of making me hide you and pretend you weren't there. You preferred your presence be kept unknown, even to me the person you snuggled up so closely to. You knew once I could admit that you were there, my misguided blame would finally be pointed in the right direction, and only the truth could begin to set me free. Because of you, addiction, I devalued myself and everyone I loved by putting you as the main highlight in my life while allowing everyone else fall into the background. My sole purpose became centered around my addiction. Everything had to lead to my next drink.

Addiction was the star of the show called *My Life*, and everything else just became extras. If I had a good day, I'd use a drink to celebrate. If I had a bad day, I would use a drink to console myself; and if I had a mediocre day, I'd use a drink to spice it up. But what I didn't know is while I made plans to use you, you also had your own plans brewing to use me and eventually take me over. You were never actually meant for any good for me. Your motives were always to strip me of the best parts of myself, taking away all I had to offer the world and making me a slave for you. It's amazing how I couldn't see your true intentions while I was caught in your grips. It's only now that my vision is not blurred by your toxic veil that I can clearly see the plans you had for my demise. But there is a saying that "whatever doesn't kill you makes you stronger!" You planned to break me down and strip me of my purpose, but I am so grateful that God's plans were more methodical and powerful. What you meant for my demise he used to build me up. Addiction, you tried to separate me from my family, but the image of me dying right before their eyes only fueled them to fight for me. And as a result, it drew us closer. You tried to remove my ambitions toward my life goals; but through my painful experience with you, it only increased my passion toward helping others not to experience the same thing. You tried to rob me of my identity; but through this journey of sobriety, I am continuously discovering my true self. You tried to take from me, but God added more to my life. He even used your destructive efforts to do it. I now have a new appreciation for living life in a sober body, free from the toxic grips of addiction. Life is so much meaningful now because I had to fight to regain it. Addiction, I don't know where you came from, but I now do know you have done enough damage. And you are certainly not welcome on the rest of my journey of life.

P.S. I cannot leave you with any well wishes, and I will no longer do you the favor of hiding you. I will use my story to help others break free from the grips of addiction and reconnect with their true identities.

My Story

I was eighteen years old, and I was freshly kicked out on my own. Back then, I and my mom were in one argument after another, and we could never seem to find the right words to reach common ground. I was officially an adult and just wanted to be cut a little slack. My mom was a strict island woman that had no tolerance for two grown women living in her house. I wanted to be seen as the woman I was growing into instead of being looked at as a little girl that needed all these rules and restrictions. I just wanted to be allowed a little freedom and for my voice to be heard; but everything I said was considered back talk, so I held it all in. My mom just wanted me to listen. Do as she says and obey her rules while I was under her roof, as she would put it.

The tension became very thick in the house between us two; and one day, during one of our heated telephone arguments, she told me when I get home, I would meet my belongings packed, waiting for me to pick them up. She said if I wanted to be an adult that lived by my own rules, I have to go do it outside of her house. Right then, a strong feeling of fear came over me because I knew I had nowhere to go, but my pride kicked in so all I could say was "okay." And later on, I went home to get my things. My girlfriend asked her mom could I move in with them. Her mom was nice enough to say yes; but once I got there with my all bags, I quickly realized they had no room for me. Staying there would make everyone uncomfortable, including myself. I knew I needed to find a place of my own. But I also knew my job as a cashier at a smoothie bar wasn't going to make moving out of my friend's house a reality anytime soon. I was stuck in between a rock and a hard place I didn't know what to do. But I certainly didn't want to wallow in my new reality, so I started going out every any time the opportunity presented itself.

I thought it was a great way to get my mind off of things. My girlfriends and I would hit all the happening party scenes in Miami, but our main hang out was on South Beach. On one of my first nights on the South Beach Strip, I met some older girls while walking to a club. They weren't dressed for the club, so I asked what they were getting into tonight. They replied saying they just came out to grab a bottle of alcohol and were planning to head back to their house to have drinks and hang out. The two girls invited me over. They seemed pretty cool, so I agreed. They were South Beach residents, so the drive over to their apartment wasn't far. Once I got to their house, they poured me a glass and unknowingly introduced me to an addiction. With every glass I drank, I became more social and talkative. Within an hour, I went from not really knowing the girls to laughing and sharing stories as if we were long-term friends.

The next morning, I woke up with a throbbing headache. I got up from my bed and stared at the floor in confusion, wondering who the heck came into my room and puked on the floor. I also didn't remember driving home. But I looked out of the window, and my car was parked perfectly outside. It was all a mystery to me at the moment; but looking back now, I realized I experienced a blackout. That night, at those girls' apartment, was the first night I drank; and even in all my confusion, I was sure I discovered a new friend that could come to be very useful in this tough segment of my life. I figured this new liquid friend could help me whenever a situation got tough or too heavy. Besides, without the shield of my being under my mom's roof, life was becoming too real too fast, so I was happy to meet the acquaintance of such a dependable ally.

We became close fast. She was a confidant. She never left me. She was the one I could lean on. I even gave my new-found friend a name. I called her "Enty!" She was like gold in a bottle. Anytime I needed courage, I would have a few shots of her in a shot glass of Patrón, and I'd be as brave as a lion anytime I needed to get away from the thoughts in my mind. I could have a few glasses of her in a vodka and cranberry mix, and suddenly be on a mental hiatus. And any time I needed a good ole venting session, I could grab a whole lady in red Merlot bottle of her and have the best crying session as if my good friend had stopped by to have girl talk.

Enty was seemingly good to me. Whenever life seemed ugly and unbearable, she'd help paint a better picture for me. I felt as long as I had access to her, I had a life-long companion. She allowed me to escape from my realities in life. I was afraid to see life as it was. Enty knew this and was good at taking me away. The more I spent time with Enty, the better I became at burying my truths. I'd gotten use to burying any thought that caused me pain. You see, I actually began burying long before I met Enty. I'd buried a secret that I had been holding most of my life.

I had been molested at ten years old. I was afraid to tell anyone, so I was left alone with the guilt and shame. I'd convinced myself that it must have been something I'd done to have brought it on myself. I thought I was too naive and that I placed myself in the wrong situation. I thought, *If I wasn't so stupid and so easy to trust everyone, I wouldn't have been in a position to get molested in the first place.* But the thought of it still hunted me. I also buried the fact that my heart ached every time I thought of the broken relationship I had with my mother. Sometimes I'd sit and imagine how much of a great relationship we could have had if things hadn't turned out how they were, but I just couldn't find the right way of communicating with her to bring that fantasy to a reality. We became so distant over time, and all the unresolved hurt and unexpressed feelings had drove an even bigger wedge between us.

On top of all this, I was constantly trying to get away from my current situation of being out in the world with no stable place to call home and no one I could call on. I feared to face all these things, so I choose not to. I buried all the thoughts and emotions. Of course, Enty was there to help me. She made it so much easier to disconnect from my feelings. Like magic, with every sip, they all seemed to become meaningless. As time went on, I managed to find a new job, a place of my own to live. My friend, Enty, stayed close to me though. I also became very good at hiding her presence. I believed our friendship had become seasoned. So like any other long-term friendship, we'd had some good times, and we also had some bad times. The more I aged and matured, I started to realize our good times were becoming far and few, and the bad times were more frequent that it was actually becoming my norm.

But I still didn't get rid of Enty. Though honestly, I became accustomed to having her around. I felt dependent on our friendship. I feared losing her so much. I found myself shaking anytime I kept her away for too long. She'd been such a faithful, available friend to me over the years, so I guess I had to be faithful to her too. Anytime she'd given me a night of fun and escape, I'd be required to pay her back by calling out of work the next morning only to throw up, sleep, and restart the drinking binge all because she still wanted to keep the party going. I lost job after job by calling out so much. She'd help me be a social butterfly on my nights out on the town. I'd meet nice friends, but then she'd consume so much of my time and would require me to be distant and pull away from my new friends to make more time for her. She was the jealous type, so I would eventually end up losing my friends. She'd help me through the tough times in my relationships but then require me to get irate with them when they'd notice her presence. She didn't like to be called out. Enty made me lose a lot, but at least I still had my trusty friend to comfort me through the pain and paint a beautiful image that everything was still okay. At least that's what I thought.

I started to feel our friendship had taken a turn for the worse, and our exchanges were unfair. She'd help me bury my pain and help me escape for a night, and I'd have to pay her back with my jobs and my relationships. I thought, *What type of friend would be there for you*; but in return, you are required to pay them back with jobs and relationships. But I feared to walk away from what I thought was a comforter in hard times. I feared life without her because I feared to feel real emotions. I feared to face and deal with childhood trauma, and I feared to be present through the ups and downs in my roller coaster of a life. Through my fear glasses, I wasn't able to see the truth that the friend that I ran to as a comforter had actually become my worst enemy that was causing my downfall. I started to realize the truth about Enty. My so-called friend was actually holding me back rather than helping me along. I had to admit that Enty wasn't a friend. She was an addiction; and I, Patra, was an addict.

So I started to take some steps to regain my strength. I slowed down on drinking, and I even attended some AA meetings. While sitting in an AA meeting, I realized I was the youngest there. I sat there afraid to share, so I just listened. I heard stories from people who had addictions older than I was. I also heard stories of people having a long stretch of sobriety, but somehow fell off the wagon and ended up being sucked back into their addictions after fifteen whole years of sobriety. Right then, fear took the microphone and tapped it to get my attention then said loudly, "You see, Patra, no matter how long you manage to stay sober, you'd still eventually be doomed from an addiction to alcohol." I sat there in fear thinking, *I just figured out exactly how I would die.* I got discouraged; and as depression settled in, I felt like I needed a drink. I felt like running back to my old friend for comfort. Besides, it was hard to give up drinking completely especially at my age when everything seemed to revolve around drinking. Everywhere I went, someone was offering me a drink, and I almost seemed to be a big letdown if I declined it. I felt like I had a choice to either be housebound for the rest of my life or a party-pooping outcast if I went out and didn't drink.

So I just continued on in life with my frenemy Enty, dragging her around like a ball and chain, figuring who cares how I'd die anyways. No one would even notice. If I was gone, I felt I had nothing or no one to live for. I struggled with being afraid to let go of something I knew was killing me, but I still held on to it because my fear convinced me that drinking was all I had. Well, that was until I experienced hitting my ultimate rock bottom.

I had been in a downward spiral of drinking for one week straight, and Enty was there to help me toward self-destruction! I was polluted thoroughly with alcohol. At this point, there was no longer any pleasure in drinking. I was drinking because I felt I had to. It hurt me to keep drinking; but I knew it would hurt even more to stop, so I kept prescribing myself the same liquid demon that was poisoning me. Enty had loaned me her liquid spirit to escape for a week; and as usual, she wanted to collect her payback. But this time, it was different. Enty seemed to be more aggressive, and she didn't seem to be asking for her normal trade. She wanted something much greater and wouldn't settle for anything less. She wanted my life! I felt it to my core as she'd made her way to invade every cell of my body in her toxic takeover. My body desperately wanted to be detoxified, but it was too late. I was already engulfed by the enemy.

Enty who disguised herself as my friend was actually an entity on a mission to claim my life. At this point, I was sick and was continuously throwing up. I had pains on every part of my body. All of my nerves were shot. I was weak and frail. My mind was rambling with nonstop wicked thoughts accompanied with dark disturbing visions. I felt I was in a tug-of-war for my own sanity. It was as if something was trying to take over my body and get rid of me for good. Enty had finally revealed herself for what she was. I knew, for sure, I was wrestling with an entity for my life.

I had nothing in me left to fight; so I knew if I was going to succeed at overcoming this entity to regain my life, I needed strength that I did not have. I didn't know what to do, but then I suddenly recalled a true friend. I started to cry because I realized how much space I had allowed to come between us. I wondered if he'd forgive me for letting things go this far without reaching out to him sooner. I also began to remember his ways. I remembered that he was faithful and forgiving, merciful and compassionate. I remembered that he was all sufficient, and his power worked best in my weakness. I knew he was exactly what I needed, so I hesitated no further. I called on him. With my polluted mind, I could barely get out a sensible sentence, let alone a prayer, but I kept trying. And with each prayer, I sounded a little more sensible.

I simply cried out for God. I asked for his forgiveness and asked that he'd save me. I thanked Jesus for the ransom he had already paid for my sins, and I asked him to cover my debt with the entity of alcohol that I've abused for so many years. Through that prayer, I felt my slate was wiped clean; and through God's saving grace, I was no longer in debt to a spirit that wanted my life. That spirit would now have to face my God to get to me. Although I was far from being out of the woods, I knew if I kept praying to God while keeping my faith, I'd get there.

In the midst of that fight, I reminisced on me and Enty's long relationship. I thought about how she snuck into my like at my lowest point and stuck so close to me for all these years. She had been on a mission to claim my life. She had plans to stop the seed of purpose that God planted in me. But I was confused all along and had mistaken her for a comforting escape and even a friend. I was too fearful of letting go of something that had no good intentions for me, so I allowed her to consume me a little at a time until she had gain full control of me.

While I reminisced on the motives of a fake friend, I had an epiphany. Through seeing the fueled determination of Enty to bring me down, it showed me the magnitude of my purpose. I realized I must contain something in me so grand and so praiseworthy that the enemy specially assigned Enty to insure my purpose never sprouts. This realization gave me a new value on my life and the seed it carried. I started to see the light beyond the clouds. Things began to fall into perspective. My mother took unauthorized time off work to be by my side. She was willing to put everything on the line, all in fear of not to lose me. All of the tough times throughout our relationship dissolved in the midst of seeing her love for me.

Nothing else mattered except love. It was the key ingredient to bringing down all the walls of defense and miscommunication between me and her. She was desperate for her daughter to live. My brother turned what was normally four-hour drive from Tampa to Fort Lauderdale to a two-and-a-half-hour drive, speeding to be by my side to make sure he wasn't going to lose his sister. He stuck by my side with no judgment, just pure love. And my love stuck by my side neglecting everything else saying, "I can replace anything else I might lose, but I can't replace you!" Wow, that's love! I felt the love of family, a love that I was wrongly convinced that I did not have. I saw that I had a lot worth living for and a lot to fight for.

I made a declaration to God and myself to never let an addiction control me again and to never devalue the valuable gift of my purpose that God designed especially for me. I choose life over death, and I choose to live in my calling. Throughout the years of living with an addiction, I've experienced what it was like to live in a poisoned, toxic body and how much of a prison it can be for the soul. A toxic mind and body serves as a blockage when trying to connect with God. It is a struggle for the soul to connect to its source while being encased in a polluted body. Being in a toxically polluted state of any kind serves as a gateway to be misguided by the enemy. By going through this experience, it is now my passionate mission to learn how to make the mind and body a perfect host to allow our soul to connect with God in a way that it allows us to be in perfect alignment to exude his spirit while we carry out his assigned purpose for our lives.

DEAR ADDICTION

I've been delivered from over a decade of an addiction. I know I don't look like what I've been through, but that just shows how good God is at restoring back what we've lost and then some. God has blessed me with a thriving life ten times over what I could have ever imagined for myself. I live knowing that in life, trials are sure to come; but through God, we can overcome each one of our trials without being overtaken by them. Amazingly I've found blessings strategically planted in each one of the struggles I've faced which showed me that God never left me. In fact, he has managed to turn every downfall into a triumph and a testimony, and I know I am a better person having gone through them. Although the enemy used addiction to tear me down, God turned it all around for my good and his glory.

Dear Addiction, in case you are wondering how am doing now, I live bountifully, pray combatively, be me expressively, think positively, speak peacefully, smile excessively, create powerfully, stand firmly, give abundantly, forgive thoughtlessly, love radically without boundaries, quit unwillingly, praise relentlessly, pray unceasingly because I am blessed overwhelmingly!

What Has Saved Me From Addiction

How I Maintained My Sobriety!

1. Prayer.

    The most significant thing was prayer! Even in times when my mind was too polluted to form a sentence, I tried to pray anyways, and I felt God meets me wherever I was. I even asked God to help me pray so that I could connect with him; and every day my mind became a little clearer, so prayers began to make sense to me. I believed they always made sense to God. He accepted my cry for help no matter which way it came out. My family also prayed for me. I know this because they told me. I didn't have the strength to get myself out of the toxic entanglement, so I knew it was from a power greater than myself. I and my family witnessed the miracle of prayer when healing took place. God heard our prayers!

2. I made a choice.

I made a choice to be free. I wanted desperately to be free from the grips of alcohol addiction. Addiction had taken me far away from the person I truly was, and I wanted my true self back. I knew it would be a fight and a long journey to regain myself, but I was ready for it. I knew there was no going back to the life addiction had for me. I wanted to get on board with the abundance of God's plans. A life filled with drugs and alcohol didn't measure up to who I could be for myself and family without it.

3. I saw the truth about addiction.

Another great thing that helped me was seeing alcohol addiction for exactly what it was. Once I stopped covering up my addiction, I was able to see it in its true form. I was able to see what it had done to my life. I saw that it was an entity with the same motives as the greatest enemy to man. Addiction comes to steal, kill, and destroy. I saw addiction's attempt to steal me away from those who loved me. I saw addiction try to kill my dreams, my joy, and ultimately, my reason for existing. I saw addiction try to destroy every part of me—my health, my mental sanity, my natural nature to be kind, loving, honest, and caring. It turned me into someone that I wasn't. I saw that it did not want me to carry out my purpose in this world. I saw that it was an enemy that disguised its self as a friend and comforter. Once I discovered the truth about drugs and addiction, I viewed it as my enemy, and I wanted to keep its methods of sabotage far away from me.

4. Replaced my old habits with new healthy habits.

I replace my old habits with new ones. I've fallen victim to picking up old habits that I've let go of before in the past. I knew if I wanted to be successful at not returning to my old drinking habits, I would have to fill the void with something else. So I took the time to think of all the situations and emotions that would normal give me the urge to drink, and I thought of nontoxic replacements. Whenever I was dealing with a tough emotion, I would get in a quiet place and sincerely talk to God. I'd surrender my emotions to him while asking for his strength and guidance to help me get through them. Alcohol was a quick fix that would falsely help me escape my emotions, but it would only end up making things worse by making me weak, not able to handle anything in life. Going to God required me to trust him while being patient and waiting on his answer. He has never failed me. I found that God helped me heal rather than bury past hurtful feelings. Going to God with my emotions also helped me build strength, and I found that I was able to handle my daily life better without getting frazzled.

One of the most common scenes that would create an urge to drink was going out to places that were centered around drinking, such as bars or night clubs. I'd always feel pressured to drink while at these places—pressured by myself and pressured by others, I'd feel the need to drink to be on the same vibe as everyone else around me. These types of scenes have sabotage my sobriety many times which is why I decided not to put myself in these settings anymore. I've created new social scenes for myself, ones that helped me along in my walk with sobriety. I thought of things that I actually enjoyed such as yoga, meditation, bike rides, joining different dance classes, poetry open-mic nights, visiting city attractions, traveling, reading, writing, etc. I went online to find groups of people who enjoyed the same things I did. I got to know myself through trying new things, and it actually enriched my life. My new activities made drinking so boring and cliché. The new life I was creating was so much more exciting, and it even helped me overcome many fears. I also joined groups in my local church. I did whatever it took to make my life look less like my old life that was centered around addiction and more like a sober, happy spiritual life. I basically made healthy padded walls for myself to protect me from going back to my old habits and ultimately, saving my life.

5. I made it clear to people that I won't break my sobriety.

I made it clear to people that I didn't drink and won't ever drink. Whenever I felt comfortable, I'd share that I had an addiction to alcohol. And that would usually stop a person from pushing me to drink. But if I didn't feel comfortable sharing about my addiction, I'd tell people that I'm allergic to alcohol, that it didn't agree with my body, and I'd get sick anytime I would drink no matter how little of it I drank. And it didn't matter what form of alcohol it was. I drew the line in the sand by letting them know this was a serious matter to my health; so by forcing me to drink, they were consciously jeopardizing my health. That would usually stop the peer pressure. In fact, they would even stand up for me if someone else offered me a drink. I didn't even have to say anything. When my friends invited me over, they'd already have my drink of choice there for me which was Seagram's Tonic Water with a lime. I stopped caring about trying to please people or fit in, because none of it was worth jeopardizing my life.

6. I created a healthy routine for my life.

I created a routine for my life. I know that sounds boring, but it kept me on a sober path. I filled my life with activities, people, routines, habits, spiritual practices, and anything else that would contribute to my continued sobriety. Replacing old destructive habits with beneficial habits helped me to stay on a healthy path. I dug deep to connect with my passions. I got to know my true self. I started valuing the activities that empowered me to be the best me, and I filled my life with those things which left little to no room to get sucked back into drinking. I found that my life is actually more enriched this way.

A Little Joke
Things to Ponder

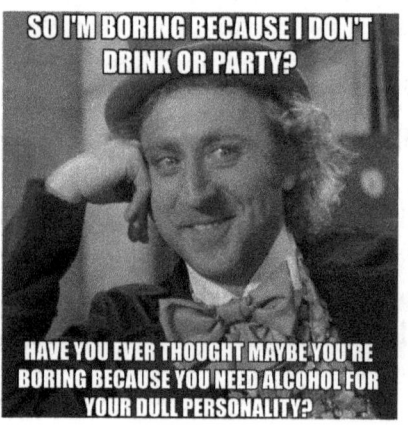

Once I became aware that the painful things I thought I'd buried was still resurfacing and affecting my current life choices, I knew I had to do something. First, I shared with a trustworthy friend; then I sought further help with a therapist. I learned that carrying around old painful baggage can really weigh on you. Even though you may think you've buried the memory, it can still be causing internal damage and can also be a blockage from advancement in life. Sharing is a vital healing tool that can give you the clarity you need to advance in life.

1. What are some things in your past that you've buried and been afraid to face?

_____
_____
_____

Once I discovered my negative thoughts were giving life to the fears that kept me restrained, I made a promise to not let a negative thought slip by without replacing it with a customized positive affirmation.

2. List three of your most common negative defeatist thoughts:

_____
_____
_____

3. Write three powerful affirmations to directly combat those three thoughts you've just listed.

_____
_____
_____

I spent a lot of time in denial of the fact that I was abusing alcohol; and within that time, I lost a lot of opportunities, hurt a lot of my loved ones, and caused a lot of damage to my body. Looking back, I wish I would have admitted it to myself sooner; and more importantly, I wish I had valued myself and God's plan for my life.

This next question may take some soul searching and honesty; but remember, there is nobody here except you, this book, and God's saving grace.

4. Ask yourself if there is a particular substance that you have become reliant on to help ease the pains of the past or to help you get through your present life circumstances?

_____
_____
_____

DEAR ADDICTION

If this question applied to you and you were courageous enough to admit that you have a problem with substance abuse, then congratulations. You are on the first step to healing and recovery which is identifying and admitting that you have a substance abuse problem. Now, the next courageous step is finding the proper help to aid you toward your recovery, then using your story to help another in need.

My Declaration to Sobriety

I, Patra Smith, choose life and all that it comes with. I choose to take all that life has to offer (the good and the bad) with no help from alcohol. I have the strength to live my life soberly. I declare I will never drink alcohol again!

What's your declaration to sobriety?

_____
_____
_____
_____
_____
_____
_____
_____
_____
_____
_____

Utilize my Heal the Child in You workshop. Go to Patrasmessage.com, select *Patra's messages/blogs* from the selection bar on the top of the page. Scroll down, and there you'll find the Heal the Child in You workshop. This workshop has been a power tool that aided me in letting go of past hurt in a loving, gentle way.

About the Author

Patra Ann Smith, born in Freeport, Bahamas, coauthor of best-selling book *Dear Fear Volume 2*, has used her gifts of writing and motivational speaking to inspire others to make life-changing breakthroughs. Patra has learned through personal experience that a toxic body can be a prison for the soul. She is a life coach who uses her passion toward maintaining a detoxified mind and body to help guide others to break free from the bondage of addiction.

Patrasmessage.com

www.ingramcontent.com/pod-product-compliance
Lightning Source LLC
LaVergne TN
LVHW090925210226
832133LV00012B/480